5-Step

Word-to-Kindle

Publishing

The Fast Turnaround Method
Using Microsoft Word and Calibre
for Quality Kindle Books
on Any Device

Sandra Thompson

Clearwater

PUBLISHERS

First published by Clearwater, 2015

This edition Copyright 2015, Clearwater Publishers

(an imprint of Gryphon Chess)

ISBN: 978-0-9943153-0-4

Cover design: Clearwater

Typeset in Palatino Linotype 11pt

This edition is printed in the United States of America

10 9 8 7 6 5 4 3 2 1

Preface

There are plenty of great guides to help you over the Kindle creation line. But if you feel swamped by the amount of information out there on how to prepare your Word document for Kindle publishing, along with all the many ways to publish, you're not alone.

You may feel like you are suffering from information overload before you even get started. While many great books show you how to wrangle your Word document into a kindle-ready file, the learning curve and amount of effort involved can take time.

This book provides you with the right amount of information you need to get your work out there quickly and effectively – and looking good too. Based on my experience as a technical writer and publisher, I have written this guide to show you the easiest, most effective way to get your book onto the sales page and start making money straight away. Advice is also provided for those who are publishing books that contain many images.

The first part of this guide takes you through the five master steps to get your work from a regular Word document to an EPUB/.mobi file, ready for upload. Each step consists of essential sub-tasks, and these methods are arranged to make the workflow as easy as possible.

The second part of this book provides background information pertinent to electronic publishing, which you may find useful, and offers a more in-depth view and steps for alternate methods for image handling, lists, and macros.

This is not another 'publish fast and make loads of money' book that only offers simple eBook solutions and a whole lot of waffle – and shows lots of images of bags of money.

Instead, this book provides practical steps, as well as unique methods, to make your book stand out from the crowd. This guide, which has many screen capture step images, also provides the best method for you to handle images so your own publication looks good on the newer Kindles, and other devices such as Apple and Android. A handy image sizing macro is also included for those books having many images – and the steps to include the macro in your Word document are provided.

All-in-all, this book is your one-stop guide to help you get your quality publication out there and start selling. Even better, this guide will prepare you for a head start when it's time to publish your book using Amazon CreateSpace, as many Kindle authors are also making money on CreateSpace print-on-demand publishing.

Happy writing, publishing – and selling!

Sandra Thompson

Contents

Preface 3

Introduction 7
   Terms and Acronyms 8
   About Microsoft Word and Calibre..9
   Free Download Locations 10

Step 1: Prepare Your Document 11
   Launch Word and save document...11
   Set your document properties...14
   Change your displayed measurements 16
   Document size...18
   Create your inside title...20
   Add a publishing details page 21
   Add a Table of Contents (TOC) 22
   Set paragraph indents (optional) 25
   Change space after a paragraph...29
   Heading 1 style with page breaks...31
   Set numbering or bullets..32

Step 2: Manage Your Images..35
   Use an image for your inside title..36
   Reset your image sizes in Word..40
   Saving your images via a photo editor 45
   Create your product page book cover.....................................47
   ...Kindle cover the easy way 48
   Kindle Cover the easiest way possible...................................48
   Image editor guidelines 49

Step 3: Save Word to HTML 51

Step 4: Convert HTML in Calibre...53
   Import your HTML file into Calibre.......................................54
   Edit your metadata in Calibre..55
   Convert your .html to EPUB or .mobi file 57
   Test Calibre output in Kindle Previewer 61

Step 5: Upload to KDP 63

    Log in and create new title 64

    HTML product description 66

    Kindle Cover the KDP Way..69

    Telling others about our new book...71

A More Detailed Look 73

    About the normal style...73

    List Bullets and Numbers 74

    What's that NCX file all about?...79

    Image compression in Microsoft Word................................81

    Compress all your images via the ribbon.............................83

    Reset all your image sizes using a macro 86

Other Useful Books 91

    About the Author..92

Introduction

Welcome to the world of fast-track Kindle publishing. Whether you are a beginner or regular author, you will find information in this guide to be invaluable.

This book covers the following five master steps for publishing, each step broken into simple procedures. The steps are:

1. Prepare your Word document.

2. Manage your images.

3. Save your document to HTML.

4. Convert to EPUB or .mobi.

5. Upload to Amazon KDP.

This is a basic guide on getting started and will take you through to the completion of your first Kindle book. This guide will also show you how to create an .html product description the easy way for your Amazon sales page.

The five main steps don't cover everything; that would take extensive reading on your part and the aim is not to bog you down during the steps. We want you to get your first book out there *fast*. However, more details are provided towards the end of this guide, following the five main steps, if you do indeed wish to delve further into Kindle formatting.

A mass of online books already cover low-level KDP development and it's hard to know which one is best for further reading. There is a suggestion for a couple of suitable books at the end of this guide, however, everything in this book will get you published and ready to sell.

No matter how skilled you are, this book should take the pain and guesswork out of basic Kindle publishing. After all, you have enjoyed writing your new novel or non-fiction book – you should also have fun in the publishing process too, and this guide will enforce you with the knowledge and confidence to publish many times over.

Terms and Acronyms

The following terms and acronyms are used in this book.

EPUB	Electronic publication – an open e-book standard by the International Digital Publishing Forum (IDPF).
KDP	Kindle Direct Publishing – Amazon's proprietary electronic publishing service for authors and publishers of eBooks.
Macro	A set of instructions (macroinstruction) used to initiate a function sequence, typically in Microsoft Word documents.
MOBI	Mobipocket eBook – a file format based on the Open eBook standard by the IDPF using XHTML and supporting JavaScript, fixed layout (typically .pdf) and layouts that reflow (for portable/mobile devices).
ppi	Pixels per inch. Used for defining image width and height in a photo editor such as Adobe Photoshop or Gimp.

About Microsoft Word and Calibre

You may ask, "Why Word and Calibre?" Word is still the most common writing tool. While other tools such as *Pages* and *InDesign* are gaining popularity, Word is ubiquitous across many industries.

You will find many eBook publishing options online if you want an alternate method for creating eBooks, and that includes Sigil and Jutoh, which have their uses. However, for this guide, we will simply be using Word 2010 (which is very similar to Word 2007), because despite what people say, Word is powerful and flexible once you know what you are doing. You may even feel you do not need to spend money on other conversion tools or word processors.

Note	Image examples are captured on a Windows computer. Microsoft Word versions may differ for Apple; however the level of setup is roughly the same. Word 2013 is very similar, although the interface ribbon is slightly different from 2010. We chose 2010 as the most common tool to base our guide on, at time of printing.

Calibre is a popular free application that handles the many conversion aspects required for a 'complete publication'. Other methods are available, including Amazon's own Kindle Previewer (incorporating the KindleGen command line conversion tool), which is a great product for conversion.

However, Calibre not only handles conversion, it's a neat tool for managing your database of electronic publications and syncing to your device. It's easy to use, and some uncommon tips in this guide will help you avoid bugs in the final output that may be generated by using other methods.

You can test your Calibre output in Kindle Previewer (which also generates a .mobi file).

Calibre also builds an NCX file for you. The .ncx file is a simple XML file. It provides the navigation notches (chapter jump points) you see on a Kindle e-ink device, located on bottom of the screen. Normally you would need to manually write an XML manifest file and then manually tag your digital content to at least every Heading 1 (chapter) level in your Word .html output. Calibre handles all this for you. An example .ncx file is located near the end of this book, so you get an idea of what's involved – and what you don't have to worry about!

Free Download Locations

If an address has changed since the publication of this guide, a quick online search will locate the correct download sites.

Calibre:

http://calibre-ebook.com/download

Kindle Previewer:

http://www.amazon.com/gp/feature.html?docId=1000765261

Step 1: Prepare Your Document

There are very few things you need to know in order to get your Word document Kindle-ready. An existing Word document can have these simple modifications done prior to publishing. You may see some steps as superfluous; however all the following tasks enforce good Word formatting practice.

Launch Word and save document

This seems like a simple task, and it is. However it is important to have decided on the name for your document.

[1]
Launch Microsoft Word and either create a new document (**File > New**), or open an existing template or document you wish to work on.

[2]
Select **File > Save As**. Save your document filename without spaces; for example, as either: 'MyDocument' or 'My-Document'. Use hyphens and/or underscores when needed. For longer filenames under a category or type, save for example as 'MyDocument_KDP-1'.

I could digress and go into discussing file structure for your kindle publications, but assume you are probably aware of how you want to structure your files. My typical Kindle document tree is similar to this Windows example…

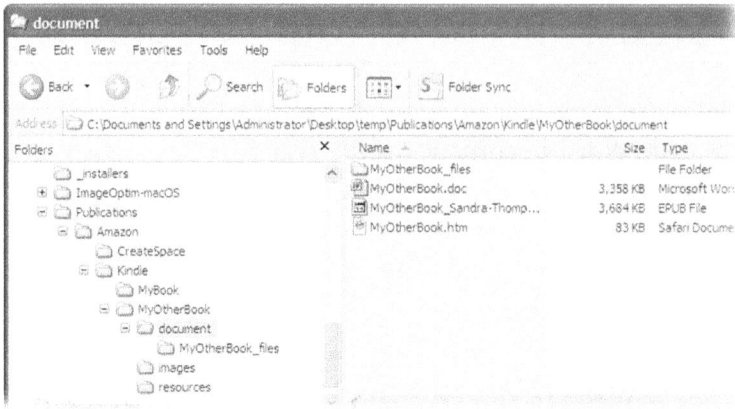

You may want to follow a similar structure. When you export your Word document, you do so to a filtered HTML type. Word typically saves in the same location; along with a folder for all your image resources (should you have images in your document). The HTML is then imported or dragged into Calibre for conversion to EPUB or .mobi.

You will notice in the preceding screen capture a separate folder for images; you could rename this to 'source-images' if you want, because if you need to change an image, you may want to keep a few versions if you have not decided on the final image.

You can also see that I have moved the EPUB file here from the default Calibre output folder where it was generated. This is entirely up to you, but I like to keep my output file together with my Word file and resources, so it becomes one-source from which to upload to Amazon – and to back up.

Also (not shown), add your final cover .jpeg image into the same location. Images are discussed in a later step, along with Calibre setup, when you are ready to publish.

Set your document properties

Some may say this is not a serious requirement; however it is nice to have the correct properties set for your document. You will find it useful when the time comes to import into Calibre as title metadata is used when you convert your book. For example, you would not want the title, *Cockroaches of the World* to appear at the top of your Kindle output – if you have downloaded someone else's Word template – and forgotten to change properties for your cook book. :)

To set document title and author properties:

[1]
Select the **File** tab (leftmost tab on the Word ribbon) and on the right-hand side under the **Info** entry, enter the title and author details.

[2]
If you cannot remove the default author (such as 'Administrator'), first add another author, and then you can delete the 'Administrator' author.

Words   2364
Total Editing Time   4264 Minutes
Title   My Fantastic Life
Tags   Add a tag
Comments   Add comments

Related Dates
Last Modified   Today, 4:10 PM
Created   1/07/2011 5   Sandra Thompson
Last Printed   1/07/2011 3

Related People
Author   Sandra Thompson

                            Copy
                            Remove Person
Last Modified By   Edit Property

Related Documents   Contact Card

Open File Location

Change your displayed measurements

We have our Word measurement properties set to centimeters for more refinement (and useful when you want to remove a paragraph first line indent, described later).

This action is up to you, but if you want to change displayed measurements from inches to centimeters:

[1]

Select **File > Options** and in the **Word Options** dialog select **Advanced**.

[2]

Scroll down; under **Display**, set **Show measurements in units of:** to Centimeters. Click **OK** when done.

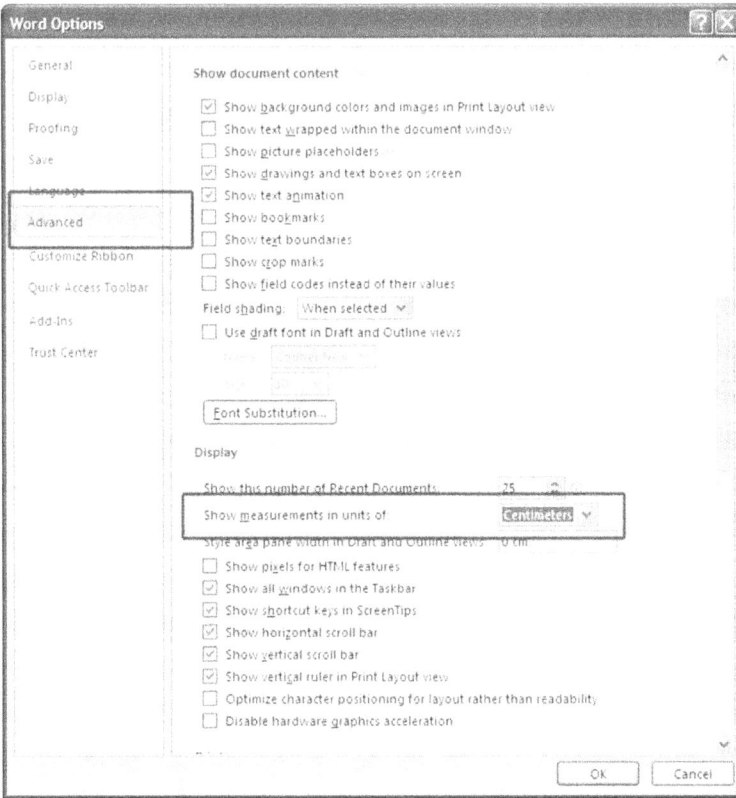

Word Options > Advanced properties dialog box

Document size

There is no required 'size' for Kindle, however for consistency, let's define one at 6 x 9 inches. Why this size? Because you may want to future-proof your book: this is the most commonly distributed book size for the Amazon CreateSpace print-on-demand service, and saves you a lot of time when you decide to do a print version of your Kindle. I publish in both, and earn good money in both platforms.

[1]

Select the **Page Layout** tab on the ribbon.

[2]

In the **Page Setup** area, click the **Size** icon, and then on the bottom of the popup list click **More Paper Sizes**....

[3]

Click the **Paper** tab and select the Custom size entry in the drop-down menu. Next, enter the dimensions for 6 x 9 inches (shown here as 15.24 x 22.86 centimeters).

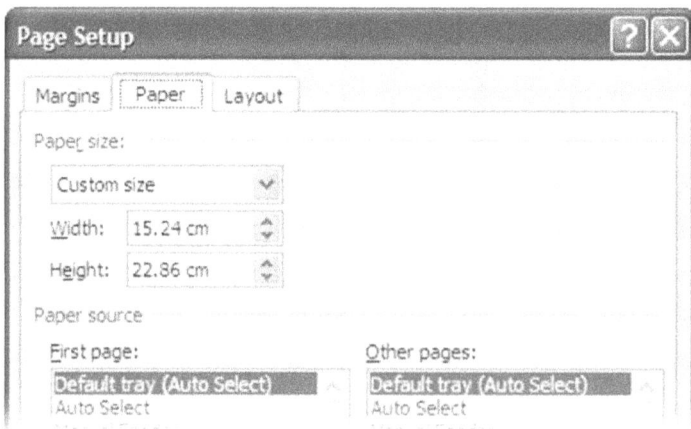

[4]

Click the **Margin** tab and enter the dimensions shown in
the following image as 1 inch top, bottom, left and right
(centimeters shown). The bottom margin can be a bit less if
you want (to allow for a page number in the footer for
CreateSpace; however page numbers are ignored in Kindle
devices). Click **OK** when done.

Create your inside title

Create a nice title for the first page inside your Kindle. You could use a Heading 2 level. Do not use Heading 1 style as this will show in your Contents, unless you want that.

You could also use an image title, discussed in the Images step.

[1]
Type the title and center it.

[2]
Click to select the title and then, via the ribbon **Home** tab, select Heading 2 in the ribbon.

[3]
Type your author name underneath; use either Heading 2 or Normal font.

[4]
On the ribbon, select the **Insert** tab and click **Page Break**.

Add a publishing details page

Having made a page break after your title image, add a page to display your publisher details.

[1]

Type in your copyright and publisher details. Later, if you wish, add your ASIN; this is the amazon number assigned for your Kindle book. Center the text.

[2]

Insert another page break. You are now ready to add a table of contents.

Add a Table of Contents (TOC)

You can either add a Preface or Forward section before adding the Contents, or add such after the Contents. It doesn't really matter, just so long as you have made page breaks between these sections. When you get to chapter sections, the Heading 1 style will have the page break set up automatically, and we show you how to verify this. If you are writing an instructional 'How To' book, such as this one, it is recommended to have more page breaks for step lists or tasks.

[1]
On the ribbon, select **Reference > Table of Contents** (icon at the far left under the **References** tab).

[2]
When the popup appears, go to the bottom of the popup and select **Insert Table of Contents**.... The Table of Contents dialog box is displayed.

[3]
In the dialog, only set the first level heading to appear in the TOC (**Show levels: 1**), and uncheck **Show page numbers** (not needed for Kindle; you can go back to this dialog later when you are ready to add more heading levels for a print version such as CreateSpace).

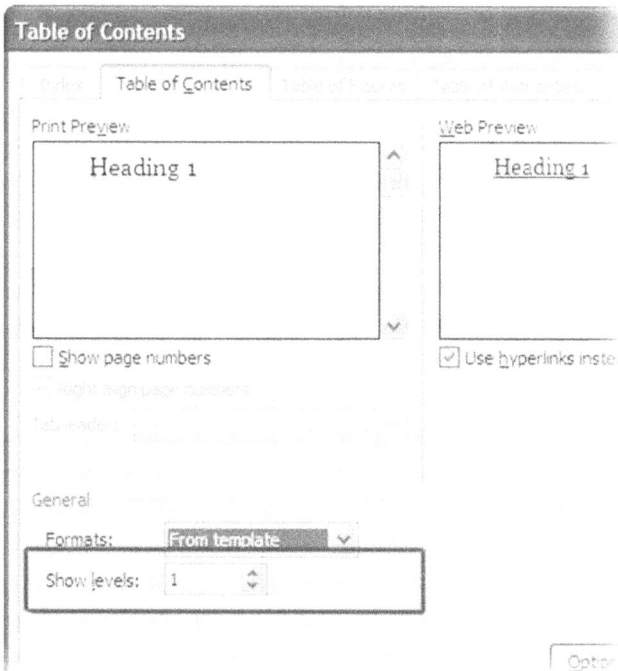

[4]

Click **OK**. Your contents will appear on the page.

[5]

Add a title above the contents to state 'Contents' and match to the Heading 1 font style, without making it a heading 1 style, so it does not appear in the contents list.

[6]

Insert a page break after the contents.

Some folks advise that you do not need to add a contents page in Word, as Calibre can be set up to do this for you (and we show you how under the Calibre steps). I like the idea of having a contents list at the beginning, and another at the end of a book. Add one at the beginning in Word, and in Calibre you can add another at the end of the document. It's a nice feature to have that improves usability and navigation on your Kindle device.

As you add more chapters, refer to the TOC and update it; make this one of the last tasks before you export your document to .html.

To update, right-click anywhere on the contents and from the popup menu select **Update Field**.

CONTENTS

Preface

Introduction

My Miserable Life

How I Turned My Life

Bullies, Money, and Pa

Analyzing the Universe

My Trip to The Observ

A Moment of Realization

One Blink of an Eye and I Make Money

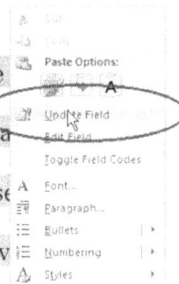

Set paragraph indents (optional)

You can skip this task if you don't mind an indent at the start of every paragraph, as Kindle automatically adds an indent.

Some people prefer indents, others do not. It's a style thing and entirely up to you. However, it is also dependent on how you want the paragraph spacing set. If you have no indent together with no paragraph spacing set, then paragraphs look like one big mass of text. On most devices, Kindle supports a paragraph 'After' spacing set in Word at 12 points. A 'Before' spacing set in Word however is usually ignored. Despite this, it's nice to have a 'Before' spacing set, so your book is primed for CreateSpace. Paragraph spacing is shown shortly.

To remove the paragraph indent:

[1]

Ensure the Styles pane/list is displayed: in the ribbon under the Home tab, click the small arrow below Change Styles. The Styles list is displayed.

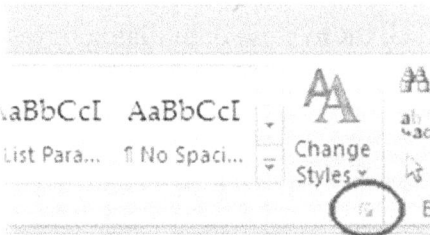

[2]

As we are using Normal for our default paragraph text, move (hover) your mouse pointer over the **Normal** style in the list to reveal a down arrow at right; click the arrow and then click **Modify**....

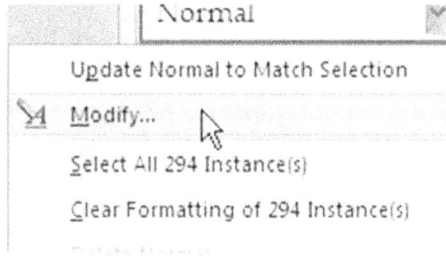

[3]

The **Modify Style** dialog box is displayed. In the bottom left corner, click **Format > Paragraph**. The **Paragraph** dialog is displayed.

[4]

In the **Indentation** area under **Special**, select **First line: 0.01** (centimeters). This action forces a new indent value, as the indent feature is hard-coded into Kindle output. By setting a new value, the indent is still there, but cannot be seen. Click **OK** to close both dialog boxes.

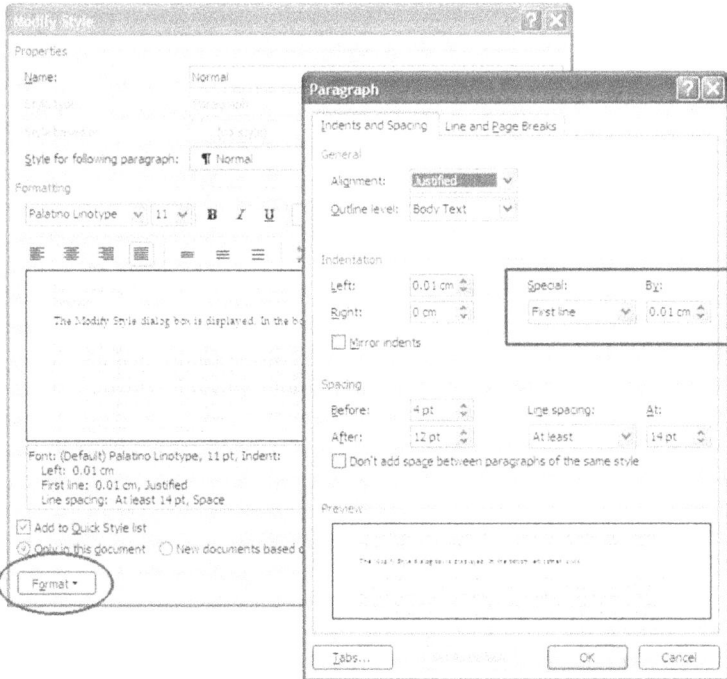

Note	If you change your measurement properties from centimeters back to inches, a zero value is displayed for the indentation in the **Paragraph** dialog. Confusing, huh?

Instead of modifying the Normal style, you can create a new style, based on normal, if you wish to customize the formatting further. This is particularly useful if you wish to assign correct names to new styles, for example, 'Normal_Kindle'. Simply click the New Style icon on the bottom of the Styles pane, shown in the following image, and don't forget to base your new style on Normal.

☑ Show Preview
☐ Disable Linked Styles

Options...

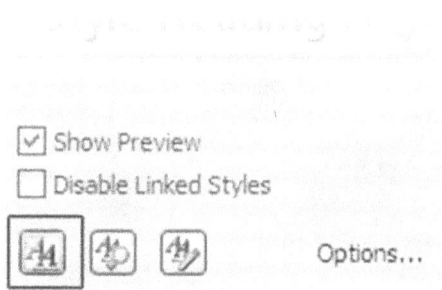

New Style icon is the lower left-hand button in the Styles pane

Tip	If you want your new style to appear near the top of the Styles pane, add an underscore before the name, for example, '_Normal_Kindle'.

Change space after a paragraph

The spacing after a paragraph is typically recognized during Kindle conversion. Add a space after a paragraph if you are not using a first line indent, i.e., your first line indent is set to 0.01 centimeters.

Note	This procedure applies if you are using the Normal style. If you have another style set already, based on Normal, such as 'Body', modify that instead – many publishers typically leave 'Normal' as is and create a new style based on it, and modify the new style instead.

For this exercise we will continue to use the Normal style. To change/verify space after a paragraph:

[1]

Follow the preceding steps to open the **Paragraph** dialog box for the selected style **Normal**.

For your convenience, the steps in brief are: click the down arrow next to Normal in the **Styles** list, select **Modify**, and in the **Modify Style** dialog box click the **Format** button and select **Paragraph...**.

[2]

In the **Paragraph** dialog box, under **Spacing**, click inside the **After** edit box and type '12 pt' (or click the up/down arrows to select the value). Click **OK** when done.

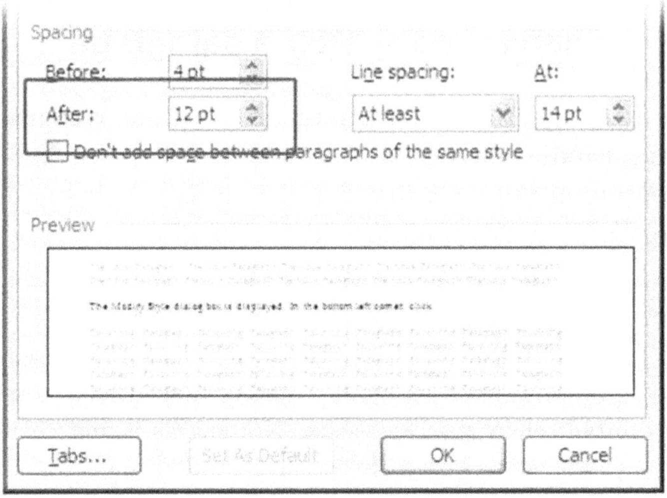
Spacing
Before:
4 pt
After:
12 pt
Line spacing:
At least
At:
14 pt
Don't add space between paragraphs of the same style
Preview
Tabs...
Set As Default
OK
Cancel

Heading 1 style with page breaks

[1]

Select the **Heading 1** style in your **Styles** list and click the down arrow to **Modify**. The **Modify Style** dialog is displayed.

[2]

Click the **Format** button and select **Paragraph**.... The **Paragraph** dialog box is displayed.

[3]

In the **Paragraph** dialog box for Heading 1, click the **Line and Page Breaks** tab and ensure the checkbox for **Page break before** is checked. When done, click **OK** to close both dialogs.

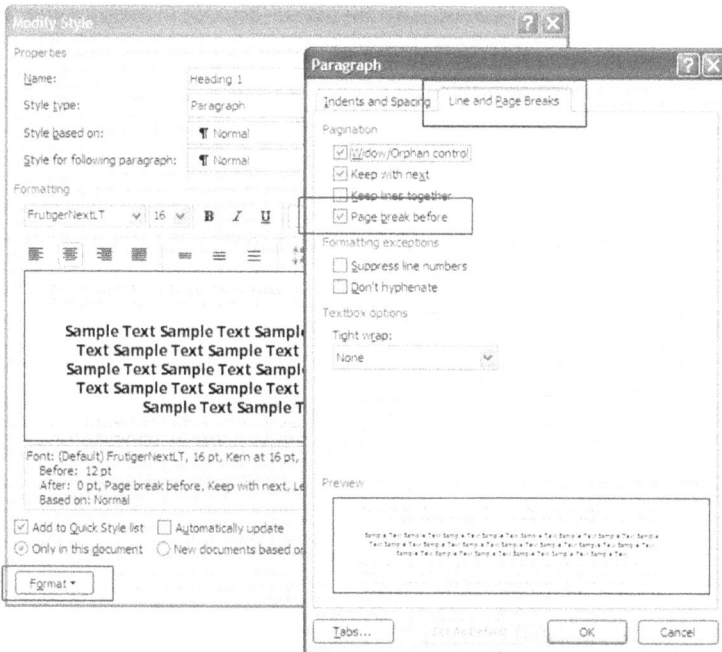

Set numbering or bullets

Skip this section if you do not require lists. Bullets and numbered lists are always a bone of contention for Kindle authors. Do not use Word's inbuilt bullet lists (using the buttons on the ribbon).

A simple method for bullets, if you have only a few words per line, i.e. not wrapped text, is to:

• Press Alt + 7 (Windows)

• Press Option + 8 (Mac)

Do this using your number keypad (or press [Num Lock]) when using a smaller keyboard without a number pad.

Ensure the list is based on Normal and left-aligned. For numbered lists, simply type a number and then a space. If you see the cursor 'tab' jump, that's Word trying to make a list for you. Simply press **Ctrl+Z** and type your fake indent space a couple of times after the number you have typed.

This method is only useful if you have a few words per line, and the line doesn't wrap. There are other methods available online for creating a 'manual' list with two or three spaces on subsequent lines, created in a Style in Word. The authors say this works, but from what we have seen it doesn't look great. It may only be effective when using monospaced fonts such as Courier or Consolas.

Ideally, we should format our bullets and numbering in HTML. An overview is provided in the chapter, *A More Detailed Look*, towards the end of this book.

In this guide we have centered our instructions. You could make them range left – ragged right – if you wish. This is an easy solution that looks acceptable across *most* devices.

However, the 'Keep with next' function in Word is ignored in Kindle, so 'windows and orphans' may still occur, meaning if you have 'Step 1' centered above each step, it may not be carried to the next page.

This basic Word formatting main step is now complete. If you wish to know more about other formatting types, there is a description in the second half of this book. Also, at the end of this book I suggest a couple of titles (by another author) worth looking at, if you want to further delve into Kindle formatting. I do not get paid for these suggestions. :)

This page is intentionally blank.

Step 2: Manage Your Images

Everyone seems to have a different take on the best way to manage images for a Kindle book. While small, low-resolution images were used in early Kindles, the newer color Kindles feature better quality images. Usability applies to images as well as navigation. If an image is too small, the reader may need to use the zoom function. This function is great, but an even better solution is to use larger images, while still having a small memory footprint.

If a Kindle book is published with many images at large image sizes, it means you as the author lose out in royalties. How, you may ask? Because Amazon takes a cut of your royalties for the book's digital download delivery size. The bigger the file size, the less you earn. There are several ways to keep an image size smaller, and these methods result in a smaller .mobi or EPUB file.

Consequently, many authors reduce the number of their images, or don't have them at all, describing a function in text only. I much prefer to use images where possible, as from an instructional point-of-view, the reader can better grasp how something works by viewing an image, instead of wading through endless text to find a few notable gems.

While .gif images have a lightweight file size, use them only for black and white line images. JPEGS and TIFF files are best for color or mono photographic images, or anything containing a gradient. When you save an image, save as grayscale or RGB. Do not save as CMYK as this only applies to books that are professionally printed.

Use an image for your inside title

If you don't want to use a heading style for your inside title, use an image instead. This will help make your Kindle stand out from the crowd. We use a simple screen capture method that works well by capturing the title text on your page.

About screen capture utilities

There are many free tools such as Snipping Tool, Skitch, pixlr (Windows), and paid utilities such as Snagit (Windows or Apple). For Apple users, there are three methods: use a free utility like Grab, Skitch, pixlr; or press <command>+<3> for full screen capture, or press <command>+<4> to select part of the screen.

You could use the <Print Screen> button on your keyboard (Windows), but you will need to crop in the image. That's why it's recommended to get a photo editor such as Gimp or Photoshop.

Note	Explaining all the many and various image editors available is beyond the scope of this guide.

Let's create an image title

[1]

Type your title on the first page; assign an attractive font (which will be used on your cover image), and then resize the font to more than 56 point (depending on how many words used in your title). Note that there is plenty of advice online about the best fonts to use.

[2]

Zoom into the title as much as you can to make it look big on your screen, and then take a screenshot.

[3]

Save the screenshot to an 'images' subfolder, inside your project folder; and save as 'inside-title.jpg'.

[4]

Open the title image in an image editor such as Photoshop or one of the many free image editors available online (Gimp, Picasa, Paint.NET, etc.), and crop if necessary. You may be able to do this from your chosen screen capture software. We use the free photo editor called Gimp. It is very similar to Photoshop and is relatively easy to use.

[5]

Open the dialog box for image size. An ideal width for your title image is 1200 pixels at 72 ppi. You could make it as wide as 1600 pixels if you are not concerned by a larger file size. More information on images is provided in a later step. Save your image.

[6]

Back in Word, remove the text title, and on the ribbon select **Insert > Picture**, locate the image and insert it. Make sure it is centered. If you don't have a centered style in Word, create one based on the Normal style, i.e., select the text, click 'Normal' and then center the image. A 'centered' style should then be created (styles are explained in the set paragraph indent step in this chapter).

Here is an example inside title .jpeg image inserted into Word. Later you will learn how to reset the image size so that it fills many different Kindle screen dimensions.

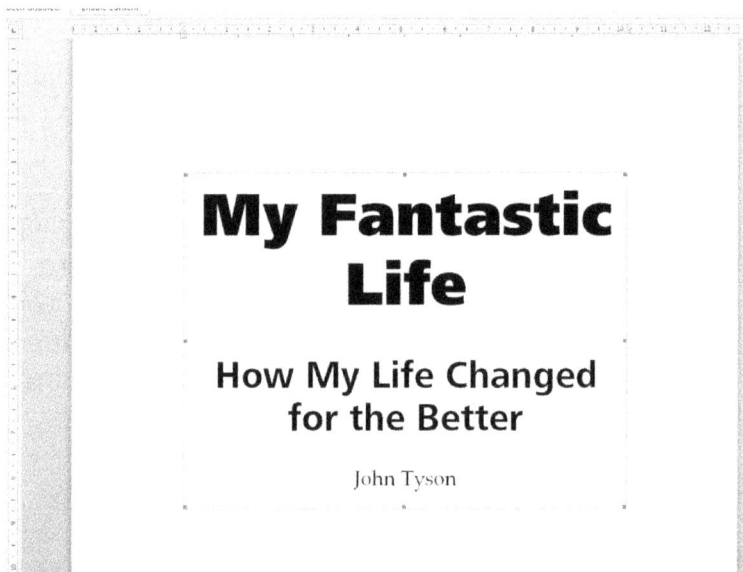

[7]

When you have inserted your title image, click at the bottom of the image and select **Insert > Page Break**.

Note	When you have added all your images into Word, there is a neat trick you can use where you can reset an inserted image so that it will be best displayed in different devices, instead of appearing small on newer Kindles. This is explained in the next step; however you will need to do this as one of the last steps prior to converting your .doc to .html. A useful macro method for multiple images is also provided in a later section.

Reset your image sizes in Word

Note	Do this as the last step prior to saving your Word document to HTML.

This is probably one of the most important aspects when using images in a Kindle document. When an image is inserted into Word, it is sized to match the bounding width of the paragraph/margin. This means the image (in most cases) is reduced. When exported to .html and converted to .mobi/EPUB, that image remains constrained at the size Word set it at. The image may appear okay on a Kindle e-ink device; however it may appear too small in a Kindle HDX, prompting the reader to use the zoom control. This is because the newer higher resolution Kindles support larger images.

To get around this issue, it is best to reset the image sizes in your Word document to 100%. When you do so, images often appear 'blown out', i.e. they become too big to see properly on the page. This has no effect on the output file, because different devices automatically scale down the 'blown out' image to fit the width of the screen. This method ensures that your images will be seen at their biggest and best. A 1200 pixel to 1600 pixel width image will look better on higher resolution Kindles, without being affected on e-ink Kindles.

Let's use the inside title image as an example…

[1]
Right-click on the image to select it, and from the popup select **Format Picture….**

[2]

The **Format Picture** dialog is displayed. Select the **Size** tab and *uncheck* **Relative to original picture size**.

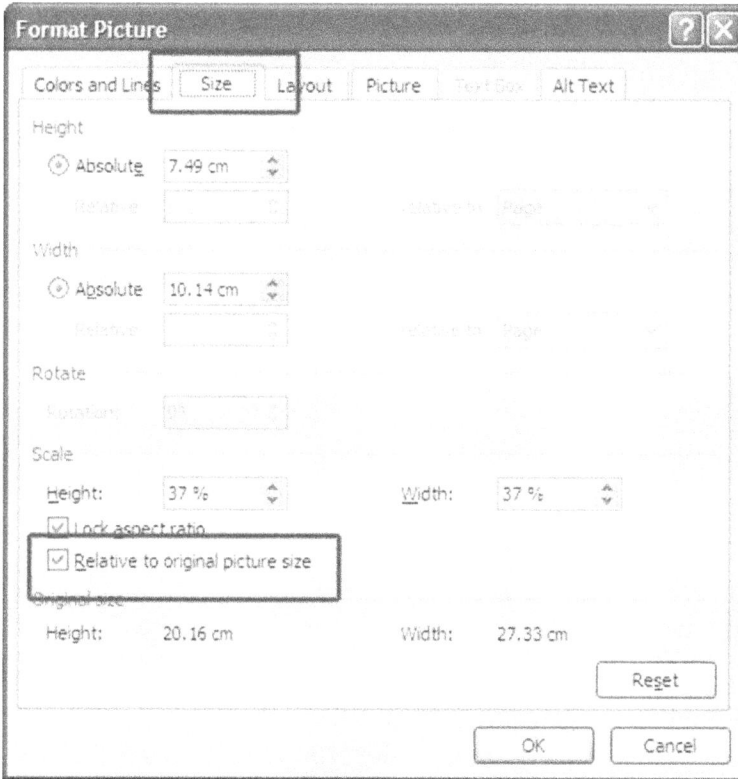

[3]

You will notice that the Height and Width values revert to 100%. Click the **Reset** button and then click **OK**.

You may see that the reset function for a large image will show the image 'disappearing' but don't worry; scroll to the next page and you should see it 'bleeding' off the edge of the page. This is normal and expected for larger images. That's why it is recommended to do the procedure as the last step before you save as HTML.

Note	If you get an error popup stating the image must be a certain size in order for the reset to occur, it most likely means that the image you have inserted is too big. Reduce the size to 1200 pixel width and try again. If you still get the message, simply hold the Shift key, click on the bottom right corner and drag the image to make it bigger, that is, drag the image so that it is stretched beyond the page edge. For example, make an image twice the size if the image is displayed in the dialog as 50% width (see preceding screen capture).

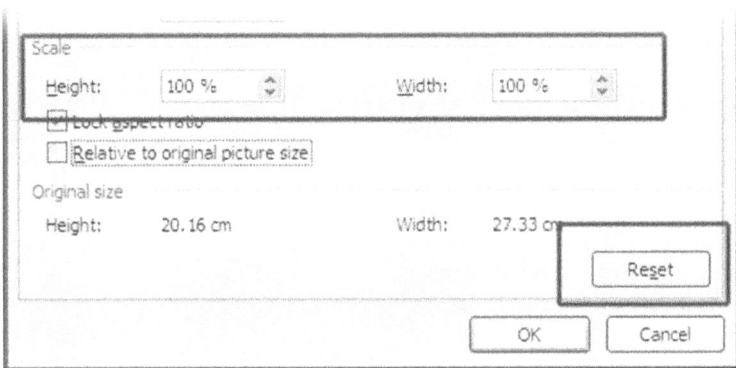

If you need to do this procedure to lots of images, a handy macro is included in this guide, in the *A More Detailed Look* chapter.

The following image shows how your title would look in the Kindle Previewer if you did not reset the image size. This example is on a Fire HDX (the image would look much bigger on a kindle e-ink device).

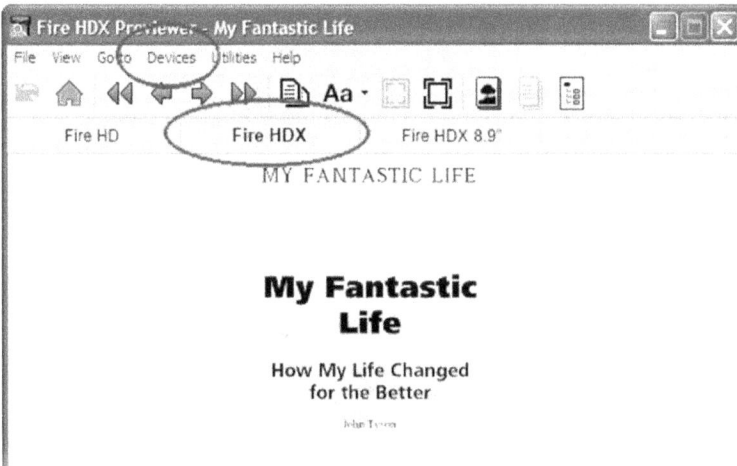

The following image shows your reset image in the Kindle Previewer, where the bounding area becomes 'floating', i.e., will fit the width of most Kindle devices nicely (depending on the size you have made the image). It will look good on Kindle e-ink devices, and higher resolution devices such as the HD and HDX. You can see why this method is preferred.

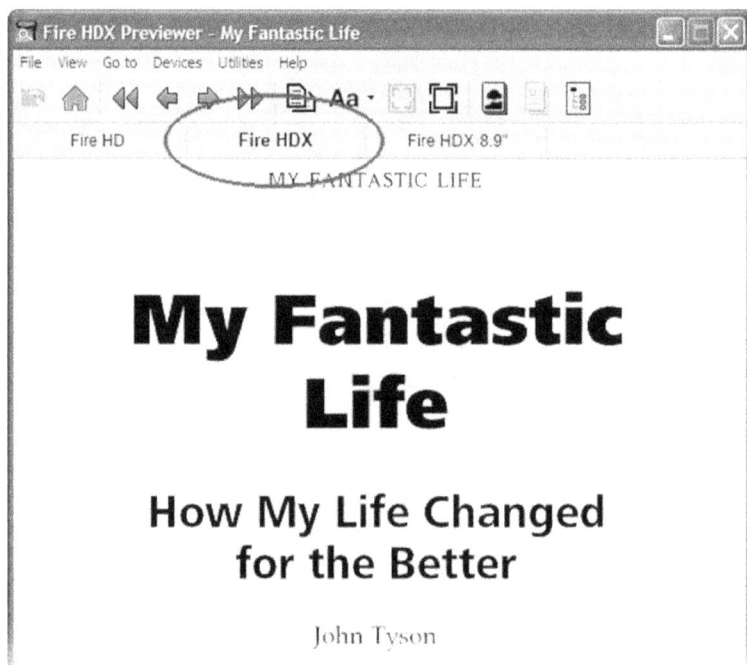

Saving your images via a photo editor

This task is prior to importing images into Word. Here, we assume you have some kind of image editor, for example the free Gimp, or Photoshop.

Many authors say they prefer working with larger images for Kindle; suggested dimensions being in the range of 1200 pixels to 1600 pixels wide at 72 ppi (pixels per inch) for images that fill the width of most devices.

When referring to computer graphics images, we talk of pixels per inch. For printing images in a paperback, we talk of dpi (dots per inch). KDP recommends 96 *dpi* and that is how screen images are captured on a Windows computer. For image depth, *resampling* and *resizing* are two different things. A 1600 wide image at 72 ppi looks fine on a Kindle. The following link offers a better insight:

http://www.webdesignerdepot.com/2010/02/the-myth-of-dpi/

Tip	When working in Photoshop or Gimp, always save a master image, preferably with layers in case you need to change title text, colors and so on. Keep the master image resolution at 300 ppi. It is recommended to save for web and devices from the master image.
	We also use our master image graphics for CreateSpace – another good reason for saving at high resolution.

When you save your images for the web, save as a high-quality JPEG. Do not save as a .png (Portable Network Graphic) as they may appear with background blocks which can occur when there is an alpha in the image (RGBA). The alpha 'channel' is the transparency channel, hence images containing transparency may not display well in the Kindle device. For example, an image with a white background set as transparent in a Kindle conversion may have the white region turned to black.

If you are converting many .png images to .jpeg, there is a handy free batch tool you can use, called Pixillion. A quick search will locate the download link. One day Amazon may officially support .png images with alpha, so authors can have colored backgrounds behind them, for example, but for now JPEG is the next best thing.

Note	You could export images at 144 pixels for supporting Retina displays, aka HiDPI, on Apple devices. We have not done this so far, but it might be worth experimenting with, because your generated .mobi file is readable on Apple devices that have the Kindle app.

Create your product page book cover

Here is a brief overview of the front cover. When you create the cover, you use it for your product sales page and typically for the inside of your book (when imported into Calibre prior to generating your eBook).

Note	The following steps assume you have some knowledge of photo editing applications. Photoshop is similar to Gimp, while others have different interfaces, such as Paint Shop Pro. Many designers create their images in 'layers', so they can edit a layer later on, and hence they keep this as a master .tif or .psd file, and export a .jpeg at a set quality level, as a separate image which is the one that is uploaded.

Before you start, I recommend you review Amazon's Kindle publishing guidelines, particularly when working with the cover image. The cover is your sales window, your advertisement to attract buyers – it is the single most important way to get your customers' feet in the door.

It could take us all day to go through the steps for the myriad of image editor applications out there, but that is not the purpose of this book. It is up to you to find the image editor you are comfortable with. There are many good ones out there and most are easy to learn. Alternatively, why not make a...

…Kindle cover the easy way

To create a nice-looking cover, you could pay someone on fiverr.com to design one for you (from $5.00). That's one good option.

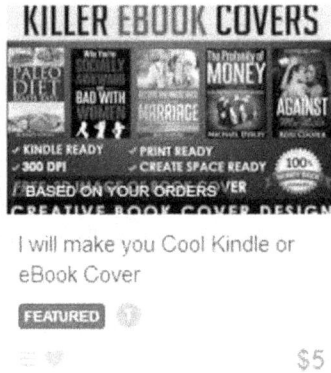

Fiverr advertisement

Another option is to buy a nice image from Shutterstock. They cost a little more but you get a professional photo that can really make your cover look great. Also, there are heaps of great Kindle cover image templates available online; simply search for one you like, download, and customize to your own requirements.

Kindle Cover the easiest way possible

If creating a cover seems daunting in itself, one of the best and easiest ways is to use KDP Cover Creator, when it comes to uploading your book. The utility has a huge gallery of images and style graphics. Please refer to the *Step 5: Upload to KDP* chapter for details.

Image editor guidelines

The following guidelines offer a suggested image dimension. Amazon recommends a width to height ratio of 1:6 which fits a typical device screen. However some people find this appears too narrow, and they use a ratio closer to the look of a regular paperback book. Entirely up to you, of course, however, on some devices your cover image may have a top and bottom gap if your image is not as tall. This is perfectly acceptable.

Many authors create a separate 1:6 ratio cover that they use for inside their book, and upload a more standard-proportioned cover for the product page.

The following guidelines assume you have some photo editing knowledge, since we cannot cover every detail of how to use an image editor.

[1]
Open your favorite image editor, such as Adobe Photoshop, or Gimp (which is free), start a new file, and save the image with dimensions 1652 pixels wide by 2500 pixels tall (longest side). Make your image dimensions 72 ppi, and save your image to your master folder containing your source Word document.

[2]
Open another image, such as a background graphic, and copy it onto your cover.

[3]

Add text for your title. Use the same font you used for your inside title. Create a subtitle and don't forget to add your author name. Be careful with long subtitles; they can crowd out your image and make it look unprofessional.

[4]

Export your cover graphic as a high quality JPEG or TIFF image. Most image editors have an export function (in Photoshop it's **Save for web…**).

Here is an example of a relatively simple front cover design done in a typical photo editor, using a modified royalty-free image. I am sure you can improve on this! :)

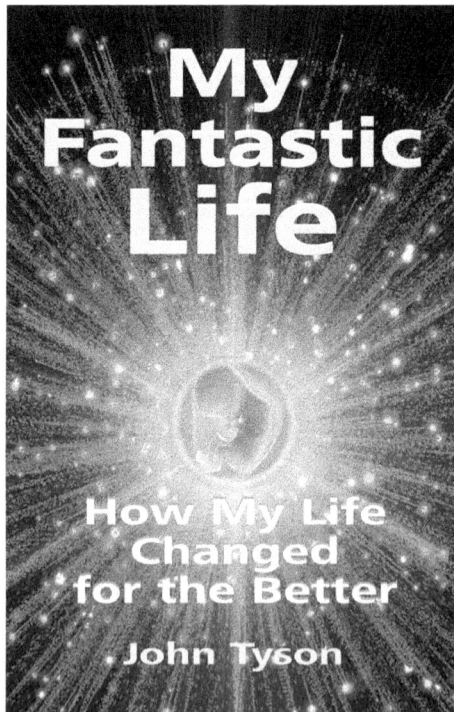

Step 3: Save Word to HTML

When you save a Word document as a typical 'web page', all the formatting and style settings are saved with the HTML. You do not need most of this, and it results in a large file with many unnecessary tags, leading to potential conversion errors.

It is highly recommended you save as a *filtered* HTML type where all unnecessary tags are ignored during the save process; and the file-size is typically smaller.

So let's now select the recommended type of HTML export to avoid those messy tags.

Note	If you have images, don't forget to perform the reset image step before proceeding.

[1]
Select **File > Save As....**

[2]
In the **Save As** dialog, under **Save as type:**
select **Web Page, Filtered (*.htm, *.html).**

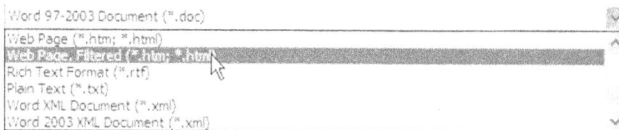

[3]
Your document is then converted to HTML, having an .htm extension. A folder containing the images from the document is also created, tagged *_files. Keep these files in

the same parent folder. You are now ready to drag the .htm file into Calibre for eBook conversion.

Note	When saving as HTML, you may get a message box stating that macros will be disabled. Click **Yes** to continue.
Tip	If you have many images, save the document before resetting the image sizes. When you save the document as .htm, you will notice the word file is converted, and presented on screen (Word 2010), while the original is closed. When you re-open the original (.doc) you will see the images have not been reset. This is great if you need to go back and make further edits – and easy if you run the image reset macro shown in the last chapter.

Step 4: Convert HTML in Calibre

When it comes to generating an eBook output, we use EPUB. You can use .mobi but you will notice the file size can be up to three times larger. Do not worry, however, as the file is split into deliverables for e-ink Kindles and Fire, etc.

File size, so I am told, can also be reduced by importing a .mobi from Calibre into Kindle Previewer and then uploading the generated Kindle Previewer file instead of the generated Calibre file. I would experiment with different file outputs and see which suits you best, compare size reduction, and ensure quality has not been affected anywhere.

Calibre is a powerful tool. For our exercise, we are mainly concerned with adding a book, editing metadata, and converting (three buttons on the upper left of the interface), plus small tweaks in Structure Detection and EPUB Output.

Import your HTML file into Calibre

[1]

Launch Calibre; the main window is displayed. Position the window next to the folder containing your .htm file.

[2]

Drag the .htm file into the Calibre workspace, under *Title*. Alternatively click the **Add books** button and browse to locate your Word document.

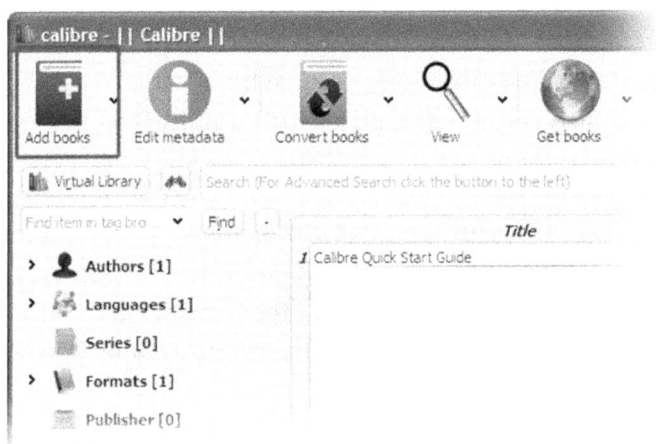

Edit your metadata in Calibre

[1]

Click to highlight your book in the *Title* list, and then click the **Edit metadata** button.

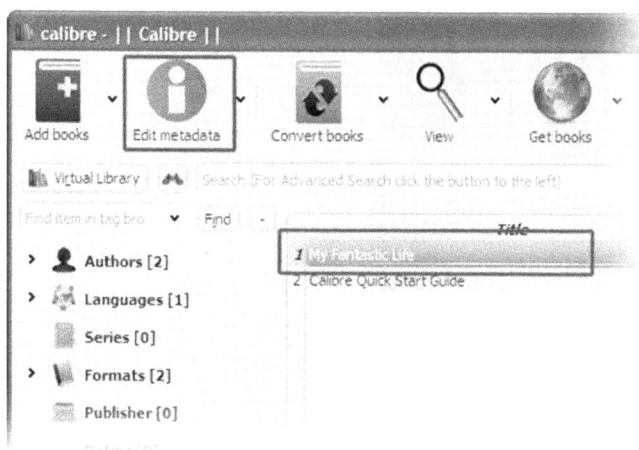

[2]

The **Edit Metadata** dialog box is displayed (and shows your title in the title bar). Add author and other information. While you don't need to do everything shown here, it is good practice and also useful for when you want to manage multiple eBooks on your computer, and sync to your device. Note that your book title will already be displayed (if you have set your title in your Word properties area (via the **File** tab), explained in Step 1 of this guide).

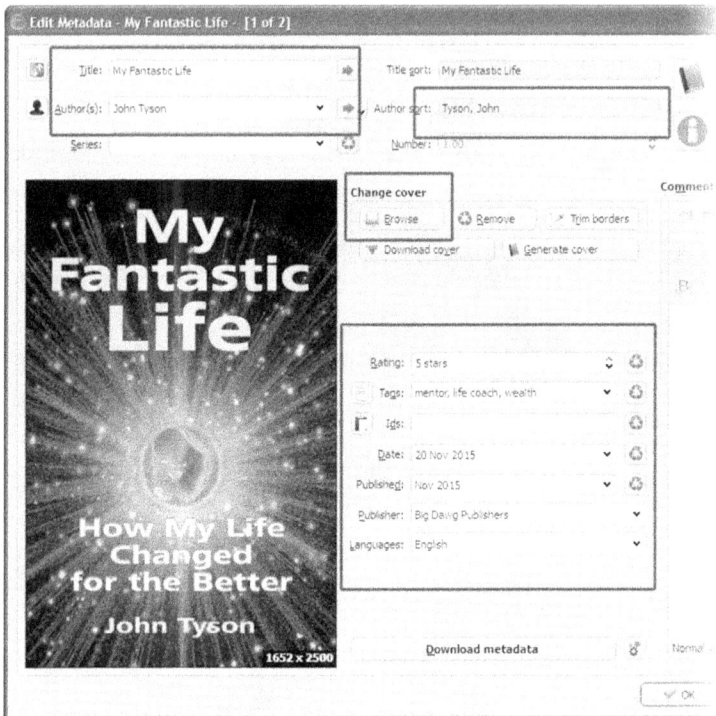

What you *do* need to do however, is click **Browse** to locate and add a cover image which is displayed in Calibre. This is the image that will appear *inside* your Kindle.

[4]

Click **OK** to close the dialog and return to the Calibre main window.

Convert your .html to EPUB or .mobi file

When you click the **Convert books** button on the main window, the **Convert [your book title]** dialog box is displayed. You can convert straight away by clicking the **OK** button on the bottom of the screen; however, we first need set some parameters prior to conversion.

[1]

First open the **Convert [your book title]** dialog box: in the Calibre main window, click to select your book title and then click the **Convert books** button. In the conversion dialog box, you can see all the metadata added to the right.

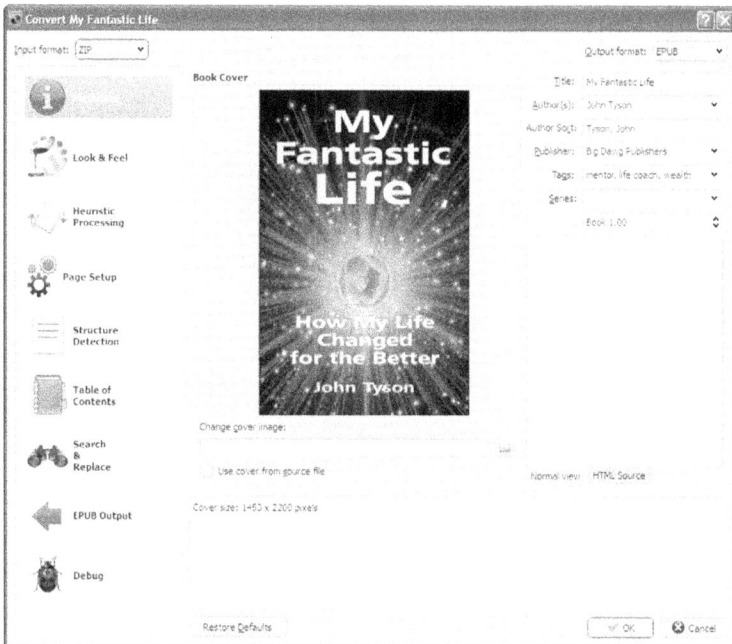

Convert [Title] dialog box

In the upper right-hand corner of this dialog box, click the
Output format dropdown list and select either EPUB or
MOBI.

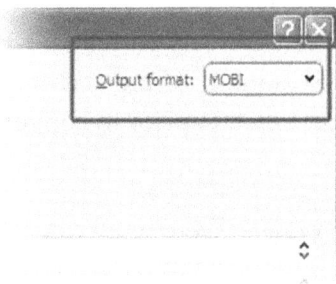

[2]

In the left column, click **Structure Detection**. Parameters are
displayed in the right-hand pane. Uncheck where it says
Remove fake margins. This action removes the possibility of
margin or alignment errors.

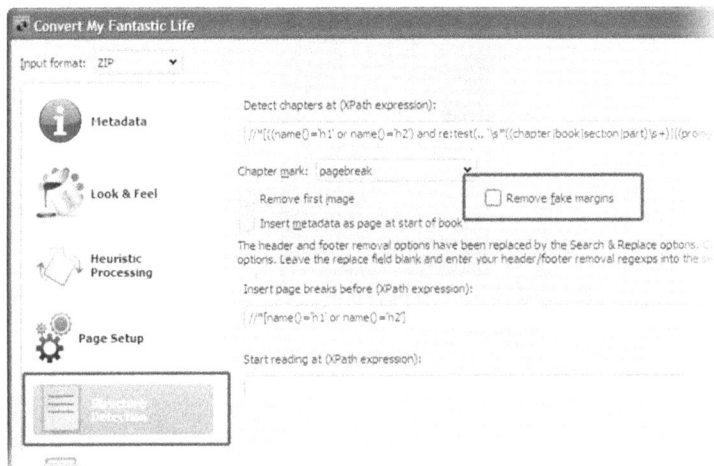

[3]

Still in the conversion dialog box, on the left-hand column click **EPUB output**. Here we will add another table of contents. First, tick the box that says **Insert inline Table of Contents**. Next, tick the box **Put inserted Table of Contents at the end of the book**.

By doing this step, you will have a TOC at the beginning (the one you put into Word) and one at the end (the one you place here in Calibre. This makes usability better for the reader. Don't forget to match the title of your contents in Word with that in Calibre; in the **Title for inserted Toc:** edit box, type 'Contents', or whatever you have for your Word .doc contents title.

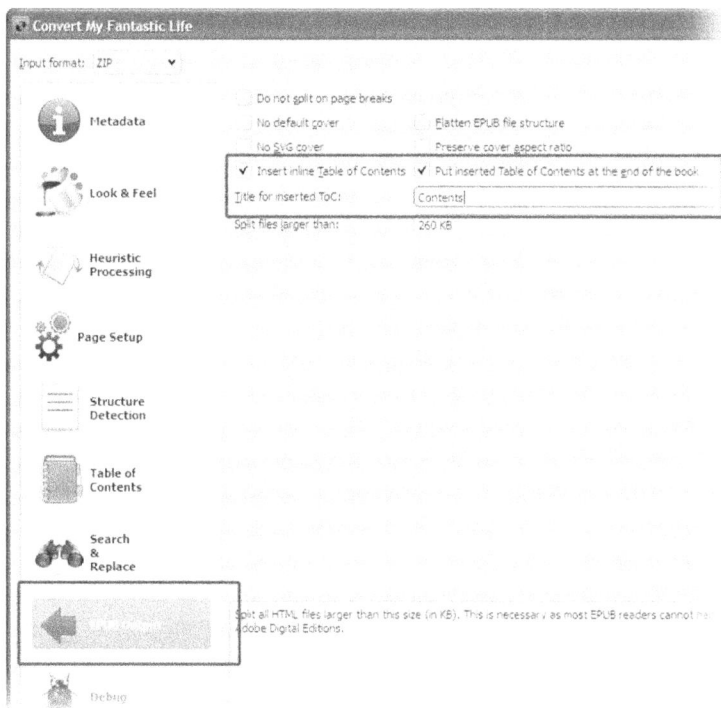

[4]

You are now ready to convert your book. Click **OK** on the bottom right of the dialog. Wait a few moments, and your file is generated in the Calibre default folder (unless you set the folder to be in another location when you installed Calibre). We have a shortcut to the folder on our screen to access the file quickly.

Note	If your document has many images, the conversion process may take a little longer.

Test Calibre output in Kindle Previewer

[1]

Locate the generated EPUB or .mobi file, Launch Kindle Previewer, and then drag the file onto the Kindle Previewer screen. It will automatically generate its own .mobi and place this file in its own converted file folder, in the same location from where the Calibre file was dragged).

[2]

Carefully review your generated file and look for errors. If there are some errors, you will need to go back to Word or the .htm file and correct. If you see blank pages, there is probably an extra paragraph return. Locate in your Word document and remove. This often occurs at the end of a section prior to a page break.

| Note | Sometimes a Calibre-generated table of contents may list additional entries you do not require. It is easy to 'filter' any unwanted TOC entries by opening the conversion dialog box in Calibre, selecting **Table of Contents** in the left pane and then entering a **TOC Filter**. Here, you can add an XPath expression in the edit box below, to ensure the heading types you want to appear in the TOC, for example, //h:h1[re:test(@class, "chapter", "i")]. The wizard lets you do this easily. Calibre is a very powerful tool; we cannot cover every feature in this book, but we know you will get to know and love the tool, and there are plenty of online tutorials available. :) |

It is wise to have different Kindle devices available, so you can actually test the document on the device. Software previewers are not always bullet-proof. Simply plug your device into your computer, locate the folder where the books are (typically 'Documents' for e-ink devices) and then copy and paste your .mobi file into the folder.

Note	Covering all the different varieties of file structures across different devices is beyond the scope of this guide.

Step 5: Upload to KDP

The Kindle Direct Publishing upload procedure is very easy to use. Amazon and many book authors describe this in detail, so we will cover this section lightly.

However we will discuss the HTML book description area in more detail, since a well-formed description is an attractive edge over the many authors who don't bother with HTML book descriptions.

I don't need to take you through every detail of explaining HTML in this section, because I will show you a simple online tool you can use to form your book description in HTML, and use the generated source markup to paste into your Kindle book description.

Note	Currently, spacing in a Kindle product description edit box is handled differently from HTML spacing in a CreateSpace product description edit box. Where you finish a paragraph, </p>, an additional space is created in the product page. The workaround is ugly, but does provide a neat final view of your product description. Examples are shown in this section.

Log in and create new title

If this is your first time, it is easy to create an account. Launch your web browser, sign up at kdp.amazon.com, and in no time your 'Bookshelf' will be ready for you to stock with your titles for sale.

When you have uploaded your title, Amazon assigns you a free ASIN (which is a type of digital ISBN). If you want a digital ISBN, you will need to purchase one from a third party such as Bowkers. All these details are explained in the right-hand column in KDP. Have the page open as you follow these steps.

[1]

The **Bookshelf** is your landing page. Select **Add new Title** to get started.

Enter book details including a book title (in the **Book name** edit box), an optional **Subtitle**, and **Edition number**.

[2]

Have your cover image ready and upload, along with your book content EPUB or .mobi (KDP accepts both types). If you have not prepared a cover, use the KDP Cover Creator tool; it's pretty good and straightforward to use, and is discussed later in this chapter.

[3]

Read the details on KDP Select; you can potentially earn more money by selecting this method.

[4]

Decide on whether to add DRM (Digital Rights Management) on your book. It is designed to inhibit distribution (though that hasn't stopped a minor few from breaking the DRM on some of our titles and distributing for free anyway) :(

The following advice makes sense when it comes to adding DRM or not: if you have a lengthy book with lots of hard work and unique content, then click the **Enable digital rights management** radio button. If, on the other hand, you have a smaller book that complements your other titles, consider making it DRM-free. Copies will become more widespread and this serves to promote your other titles.

[5]

The rest of the details on this page are self-explanatory. There is a product description to fill out and in the next section of this guide, learn how to do this in HTML, prior to continuing to the Rights & Pricing page, otherwise simply type your description in the edit box.

Click **Save and Continue** to go to the **Rights & Pricing** page. This page is also self-explanatory. Make sure you agree to Amazon terms and conditions. You are now set up for selling your title. Congratulations!

HTML product description

To make your product description stand out, use an HTML description. The HTML is simple to create. But if you don't like editing in HTML, there is a free online editor here:

http://www.quackit.com/html/online-html-editor/

Simply write your product description in the edit box, apply the styles using the toolbar above (bold, italic, bullets etc.) and then click the **Source** button to view the HTML code. Copy this code into your Kindle product description edit box.

The following image capture shows an example product description.

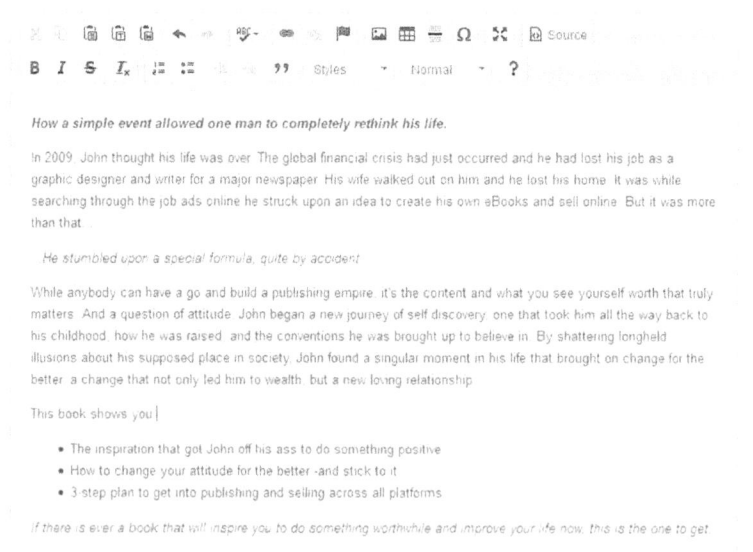

The following example shows the generated HTML. Go through the source markup carefully, and if you see odd space tags, remove them (this can happen if there is an apostrophe, for example).

If you are writing a description for a CreateSpace book, remove the extra paragraph returns so there are no white spaces between the paragraphs.

The Kindle product description edit box is a little different from the one in CreateSpace...

[1]
Paste your HTML code into the product description edit box.

[2]
Remove the extra paragraph space so that one paragraph is adjacent to the next. Otherwise unwanted spaces will show up on your Kindle product sales page, even though you don't have them in your code.

Typing it up this way results in messy looking markup for the Kindle product page, but will look fine in the resulting sales page. So be sure you have every detail you want in the description correct before you proceed to the rights and pricing page. It is recommended to clean up your description in a separate text editor first, before pasting into the Kindle product description.

Your product description markup in the Kindle edit box should look like the following image, prior to submission:

Note	A Heading 2 level in Amazon will result in the Amazon orange style being displayed.
	If you have issues formatting a HTML book description, be sure to view the various online forums about book descriptions in Kindle, as Amazon are continuously improving how things are done, and sometimes a feature may be changed or omitted.

All-in-all, it is worthwhile doing your product description in HTML. After a while you will get so used to working with the markup direct you will remember all the styles and do it manually. Seriously!

Kindle Cover the KDP Way

One of the best and easiest ways to design a cover is to use Kindle Cover Creator. The utility has a huge gallery of images and style graphics.

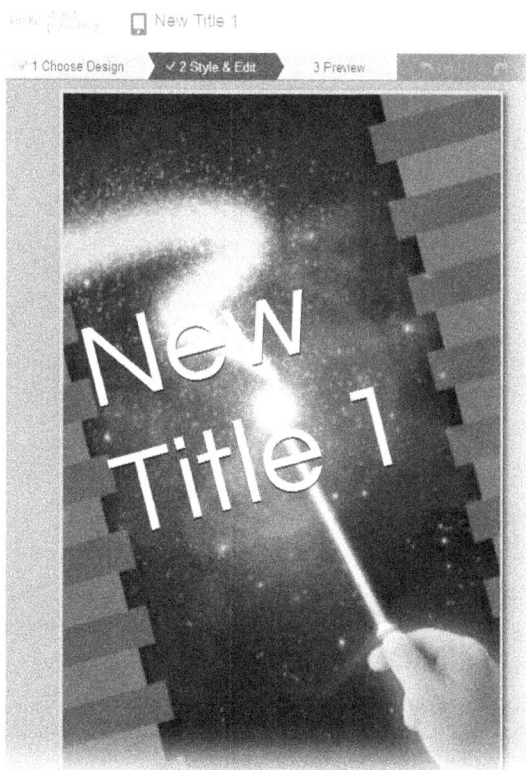

The issue here is that by the time you get to upload your book to KDP, you would have already added a cover to the inside of your Kindle, prior to the upload process (when you set up Calibre). The following steps provide a workaround if you prefer a Kindle Cover Creator design.

[1]

On the Publishing Details page in KDP, launch Kindle Cover Creator, select an image and add your text.

[2]

When you are happy with the design, go to the **Preview** tab to view your final image, right-click on the image in preview mode and from the popup select to save the image to your computer.

[3]

Next, save the publishing process as a draft.

[4]

Place your new cover into Calibre, generate EPUB, test how it looks in Kindle Previewer, and then return to KDP to complete the publishing process.

Note	When you use Kindle Cover Creator, the image size displayed is 3572 x 4896 pixel width. When you save from the Preview window, the image is saved to your computer at 1588 x 2525 pixel width (at 110 ppi). This is acceptable for inserting into Calibre for your inside image. Calibre also optimizes your inside cover image when it is generated, so the file size may be smaller.

More about Kindle Cover Creator:

https://kdp.amazon.com/help?topicId=A1DHGMW609HBI8

Telling others about our new book

There are many, many ways to promote your title; social media, blogs, your own WordPress website that complements your books, forums of like-minded people, and much more.

Amazon has a wealth of guides on marketing and promoting your Kindle title. If you find a book you like on marketing your Kindle, just be sure to read all the *constructive* reviews for particular books that may interest you.

The best first place to promote your book is via your immediate friends. Ask for an honest review of your book, provided they purchase the title, and then 'Verified purchase' is displayed.

Do not, however, pay someone for positive reviews. You will see many books with glowing, often lengthy, positive five star reviews. Most people don't have time to write a lengthy review, unless they are put up to the task, i.e., paid, so if you see a book with loads of lengthy five star reviews, my guess is to be a little suspicious.

This page is intentionally blank.

A More Detailed Look

The information on the following pages takes a closer look at Kindle development. This is not a complete look; more of a summary. There are many great guides on Amazon that discuss the subjects in this section, in even more detail.

About the normal style

The style 'Normal' in our context is Palatino Linotype 11pt (this font can be seen on some Kindles); however it doesn't matter for Kindle publishing in general as a Kindle will use its own fonts. You could use Times New Roman if you wanted to. We use Palatino because it is easy-on-the-eye, and also attractive in CreateSpace books. Calibri is a good choice too.

I quite like the original Kindle default font, that being PMN Caecilia, a slab serif font. Amazon has worked hard to get the right kind of reading font on their devices, given the available technologies over the years. On some devices you can change the Kindle reading font (the new Paperwhite Kindle offers a choice of fonts, for example); however we have not found the need to.

Also you will see that we prefer justified text in our Kindle. This is set via the **Styles** pane we used in an earlier step. Many writers use ragged right, where the column is flush on the left, and uneven on the right. This is fine for ordered or unordered lists. For paragraph text, the traditional approach is justification. It is not ideal in a Kindle transform, where hyphens are not automatically inserted (resulting in wider gaps in some places, or justify right misalignment below a minimum character-per-line threshold). Still, we believe it is a neater overall solution than a book containing all ragged right text.

List Bullets and Numbers

Do not use Word's inbuilt bullet lists (by using the buttons on the ribbon). Here are alternative methods for creating bullet and number lists.

The first method shows you how to save and edit the HTML file from Word. You use tags for a <ul> which is an unordered (bullet) list, or <ol> which is an ordered list consisting of numbered entries. Within each list is a <li> which is a list item. The following example is for a bullet list.

Create an HTML bullet list

[1]
In Word, click **File > Save As** to invoke the **Save As** dialog box.

[2]
Click the down arrow next to the **Save as type:** edit box, and select **Web page, filtered (.htm, .html)**. You will see that your document name is in the edit box above; and hopefully has no spaces in the filename. By choosing a filtered version you are not including many unnecessary tags that Word would otherwise put there – essentially you get a 'cleaner' version.

[3]

Launch your text editor such as Notepad. We use Notepad ++ which is an excellent free editor. Open the .htm file you created (you can also right-click (Windows) and select which application you wish to open the .htm file with).

[4]

In the .htm document, type the following code where you want the bulleted list to appear:

```
<ul>
  <li>Item 1</li>
  <li>Item 2</li>
  <li>Item 3</li>
</ul>
```

[5]

Save and close the .htm file when done. It is recommended to save as another version for comparison.

Note	To help you locate where to add the list, simply add heading text in Word before the list you wish to add, and you can then search for it easily in the generated HTML.

Here is an example list created in Notepad ++.

```
<ul>
  <li>Do this (<strong>File > New</strong>) thing.<
  <li>Do that <strong>File > Save As</strong> thing
  <li>Do some other thing. Blah blah Blah blah Blah
  Blah blah Blah blah Blah blah Blah blah Blah blah
</ul>
```

If you want to cut the time it takes to write html, there is a handy online converter, where you can copy the source into your .htm file. Go to the following location and try it out, (if you haven't done so already for your Kindle product description):

http://www.quackit.com/html/online-html-editor/

Even if you have spent hours setting up your lists in HTML, you may need to edit another section in your document later, which means either continue with the HTML, or go back to the Word doc, edit, and then convert again. Save all your html lists in a separate file if you do this.

Tip	You can edit the Calibre generated source .htm, located in the .zip file created when you generated the EPUB or .mobi. If you have WinZip, open the zipped folder, drag out the .htm to the parent folder, edit in Notepad and then drag back into the zipped folder, overwriting the old version. You can then easily regenerate the EPUB or .mobi.

Here is an example image showing our .htm list in Kindle Previewer. Our result is at the top. Also, below our markup, is a list created using the Word ribbon (circled indents) for comparison. When you use Word's built-in list tool you usually get unwanted indents and alignment.

2. Do that File > Save As thing. blah blah blah blah blah blah Blah blah Blah blah Blah blah Blah blah.

3. Do some other thinng.

- Do this (**File > New**) thing.
- Do that **File > Save As** thing.
- Do some other thing. Blah blah Blah blah Blah blah Blah blah Blah blah Blah blah Blah blah Blah blah Blah blah Blah blah Blah blah Blah blah Blah blah.

1. Launch Microsoft Word and either create a new document (**File > New**), or open an existing template or document you wish to work on.

2. Select File > Save As.

Do you really want traditional lists?

Traditional list formatting is not always ideal because we are supporting many different devices. Experienced folks write extensive .css (cascading style sheets) to define their font classes; many write HTML from scratch. For new publishers this may seem like too much work.

For many publishers not experienced in HTML, it is often best not to take a formatting risk, but instead use a more creative method – and we often do it too; using images for list numbers, and centering the list items. This works especially well for step-by-step instructions and results in step tasks that look neat across all devices, while adding a touch of uniqueness. Simply add an image graphic that is a number (from a set of number graphics you have saved), and have centered or paragraph text underneath. Number and button graphics can be found in many places online.

For basic lists or steps, you could use a simple **bold, centered** style above every step, based on Normal, as we have done for the Kindle version of this book. It results in a more robust and attractive Kindle output, in our humble opinion, though some may think that's a matter of opinion. No harm in trying though!

What's that NCX file all about?

NCX (Navigation Control file for XML) is a type of XML file that identifies a string tagged to the headings in an HTML file; output from Word (typically tagged to H1 and sometimes also H2). It essentially creates the navigation jump points you see on the bottom of the e-ink Kindle screen. Luckily, Calibre builds the NCX file for you.

We used to use Mobipocket Creator, and manually wrote our XML manifest files and tagged every Heading 1 level manually in our HTML file, along with writing a separate .xml pointer file. It was a fair chunk of work to do, but very worthwhile for users of e-ink Kindles.

Many authors do not bother with the NCX, and many other devices don't show it anyway. However, it is still a nice thing to have, to support the many millions of Kindle e-ink devices out there.

Here is an example XML manifest file (part shown) – and you thought writing a HTML <ol> was no fun!

```
1    <?xml version="1.0" encoding="UTF-8"?>
2    <?xml-stylesheet type="text/css" href="text.css"?>
3    <!DOCTYPE ncx PUBLIC "-//NISO//DTD ncx 2005-1//EN"
4    "http://www.daisy.org/z3986/2005/ncx-2005-1.dtd">
5    <ncx xmlns="http://www.daisy.org/z3986/2005/ncx/"
6    version="2005-1" xml:lang="en-US">
7    <head>
8    <meta name="dtb:uid" content="uid"/>
9    <meta name="dtb:depth" content="1"/>
10   <meta name="dtb:totalPageCount" content="0"/>
11   <meta name="dtb:maxPageNumber" content="0"/>
12   </head>
13   <docTitle><text>My Fantastic Life - Volume
     1</text></docTitle>
14   <docAuthor><text>Tyson, John</text></docAuthor>
15   <navMap>
16   <navPoint id="mpb_toc_0" playOrder="1">
17   <navLabel><text>Title Page</text></navLabel>
18   <content src="FINAL_MyFantasticLife_vol-1.html#start"/>
19   </navPoint>
20   <navPoint id="toc" playOrder="2">
21   <navLabel><text>Table of Contents</text></navLabel>
22   <content src="mbp_toc.html"/>
23   </navPoint>
24   <navPoint id="mbp_toc_1" playOrder="3">
25   <navLabel><text>Childhood Misconceptions</text></navLabel>
26   <content src="FINAL_MyFantasticLife_vol-1.html#Ch1"/>
27   </navPoint>
28   <navPoint id="mbp_toc_2" playOrder="4">
29   <navLabel><text>School Bullies Don't Get What They
     Want</text></navLabel>
30   <content src="FINAL_MyFantasticLife_vol-1.html#Ch2"/>
31   </navPoint>
32   <navPoint id="mbp_toc_3" playOrder="5">
33   <navLabel><text>Never Hide in the Shadows</text></navLabel>
34   <content src="FINAL_MyFantasticLife_vol-1.html#Ch3"/>
35   </navPoint>
36   <navPoint id="mbp_toc_4" playOrder="6">
37   <navLabel><text>New Money Machine</text></navLabel>
```

NCX manifest file markup (part shown)

Image compression in Microsoft Word

Microsoft Word has an often-ignored feature where you can actually modify an image from within Word. When images are inserted into Word using the **Insert > Picture** function, the image is actually embedded in Word. That means you can compress them, or make them gray scale, change their brightness, and contrast, without affecting the source image.

The recommendation, however, is not to use Word's inbuilt image editing features, preferring Adobe Photoshop or Gimp, since photo editing software offers better results with more refined options.

Word's image compression algorithm is not bad, and useful if you do not have Photoshop or Gimp or another image editor.

Also, your images may already be automatically compressed when inserted. If you have only a few images in your book, you can choose to uncheck Word's image size/quality reduction 'feature' as follows:

[1]

Click the **File** tab and select **Options**. The **Word Options** dialog box is displayed. In the left column, select **Advanced.**

[2]

Scroll down to the **Image Size and Quality** area, select your current document if it is not displayed, and then check **Do not compress images in file**.

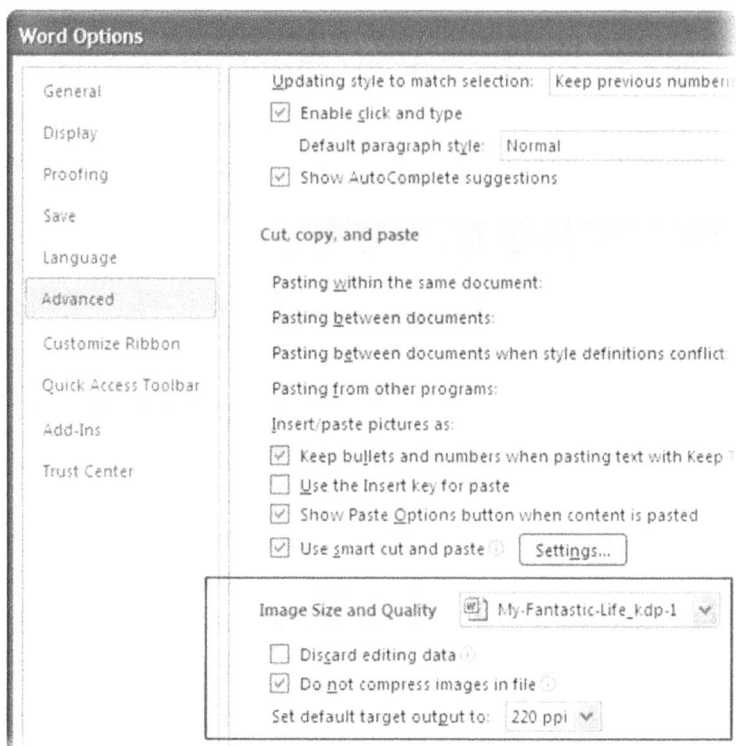

This step is particularly useful if you are importing high resolution images into your CreateSpace version. For Kindle files having many images, you may prefer to keep the compression option, or set another value.

Compress all your images via the ribbon

If you have many large images, use this option as one of the last steps before you save your Word document to HTML. This action can be done for all images at the same time, to reduce the output file size. If you only have a few small images, skip this step.

The compress action does not affect the image source folder, only the images you have embedded in your document (which are output to a separate image source folder when the HTML is generated).

While you can save a JPEG with a set compression level via Photoshop (and we do this often with a setting of 'High') by using Photoshop's 'Save for web' method, it is sometimes better to save a full-quality JPEG or TIFF file, and compress the images in Word all in one go. This means you can use the full-quality images for other things, such as a separately-saved CreateSpace version (note the recommended print resolution is 300dpi for color and 600dpi for mono).

Let's squish all images in one go...

[1]

Click to select any image in your document. You will see **Picture Tools** highlighted on the ribbon. Click the **Format** tab below it.

[2]

To the left of the Format ribbon, click **Compress Pictures**. The **Compress Pictures** dialog is displayed (this dialog may be different depending on which version of Word you have).

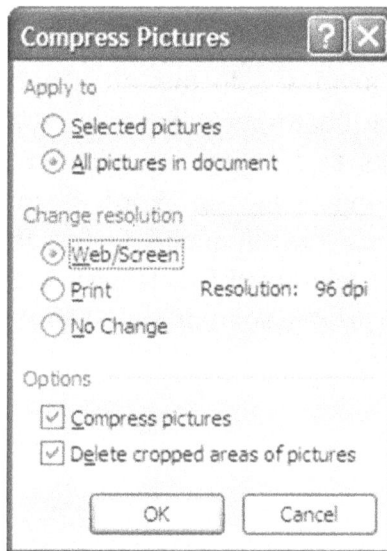

[3]

Select 'All pictures in document' and 'Web/Screen'. The '96 dpi' value is acceptable. Click **OK** when done. 'Compress pictures' is checked here. Experiment by leaving this unchecked and compare your document file size.

Further reading on compression

Amazon has image compression guidelines on their website…

https://kdp.amazon.com/help?topicId=AQY9VBML4LKPK

Also, Microsoft has extensive image compression guidelines…

http://office.microsoft.com/en-us/powerpoint-help/reduce-the-file-size-of-a-picture-HA010192200.aspx

Reset all your image sizes using a macro

This step is to allow your larger images to fit the width of any device screen, instead of being constrained by the margin in your Word document. In an earlier step, you learned how to reset an image size in your Word document. If you have many images, this handy macro will save you a lot of time as Word does not feature a global function in this regard.

Note	Do this as the very last step before saving your document as HTML.

[1]

Click the **View** tab on the ribbon, and then click **Macros**.

[2]

The **Macros** dialog is displayed; in the **Macro name:** edit box, type 'AllGraphicsTo100', and then click the **Create** button.

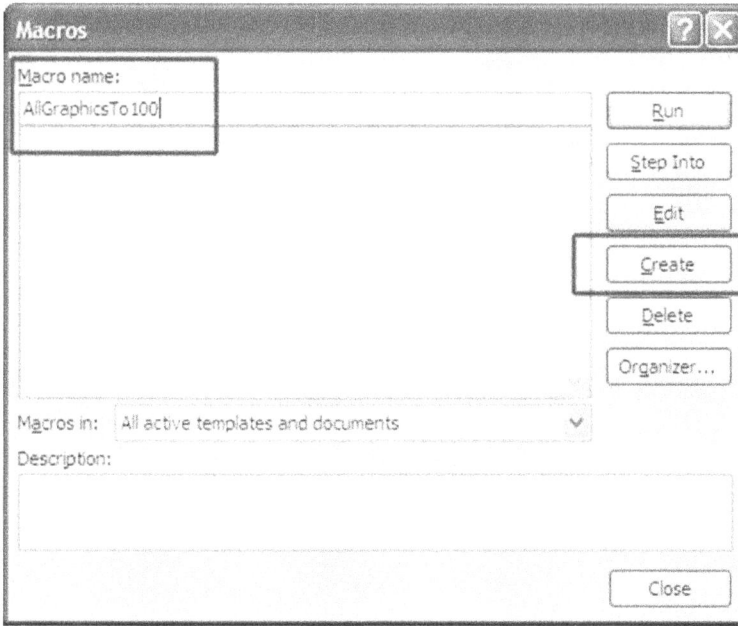

[3]

The Microsoft Visual Basic window is displayed. Copy the following code and paste into the Visual Basic edit window, and then press **Ctrl+S** to save the macro.

Macro text to paste into the Visual Basic editor

```
Sub AllGraphicsTo100()
  Dim ILS As Word.InlineShape
  Dim SHP As Word.Shape
  For Each ILS In ActiveDocument.InlineShapes
    If ILS.Type = wdInlineShapePicture Then
        ILS.ScaleHeight = 100
        ILS.ScaleWidth = 100
    End If
  Next ILS

  For Each SHP In ActiveDocument.Shapes
    If SHP.Type = msoPicture Then
        SHP.ScaleHeight 1#, True
        SHP.ScaleWidth 1, True
    End If
  Next SHP
End Sub
```

How it looks in the editor

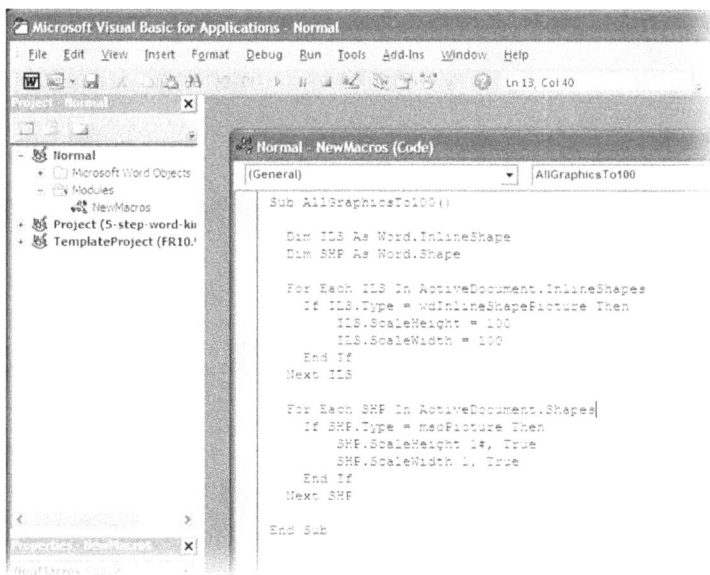

[4]

Close the entire Visual Basic editor window: click [**X**] in the upper right corner. You are returned to the Word document where you will run the macro.

[5]

In Word, click on an image to select it and then click the **Macros** button to display the **Macros** dialog again.

[6]

In the **Macros** dialog, make sure 'AllGraphicsTo100' is selected and then click the **Run** button. Every image in your document is then reset.

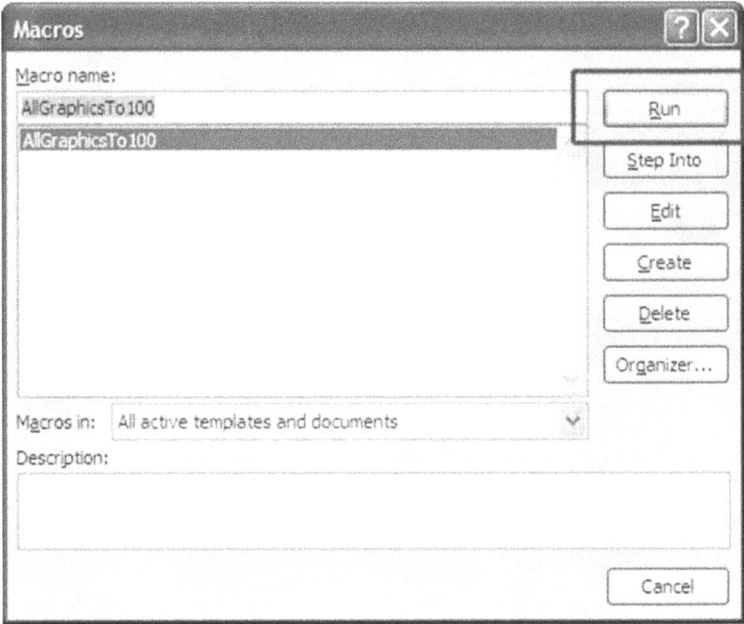

Note	If you get an error when copying the macro text from this guide, try pasting it into a text editor first (Notepad or Notepad++ for example) in case you need to tidy up the mono-spaced text alignment; then, copy it from the text editor and paste into the Visual Basic editor.

Other Useful Books

It would be remiss of me not to suggest a couple of other useful Kindle publishing guides. Rather than placing a hyperlink here that could go out of date, simply search online for *From Word to Kindle* and *HTML Fixes for Kindle* by Aaron Shepard. These books offer a more in-depth look into the workings of Kindle formatting, text alignment, fonts, and so on – useful if you want to do more serious Kindle development. And I don't get paid a dime for that advice!

About the Author

Sandra Thompson was a long-time publisher in traditional markets, working in magazines and books. With her background in graphic design, computing, and technical writing, she was well-experienced in the production of quality publications for children and adults.

Approaching retirement age but not quite ready to retire, she was given the pink slip. Sandra was not deterred and now she runs her own publishing and graphics business, helping others to get published in the online world. "I wouldn't go back to a day job," she states happily, "...especially working for a pointy-headed manager."

Her words of advice for anyone entering the world of digital publishing are clear: "Define an area of need in the market, learn about it, and fill it – and keep learning. In everything you do, you can only be honest with your customers if you are first honest with yourself. Follow this simple advice and you will go far."